The Workbook Self-Care Self-Love for Overwhelmed Moms Copy

Practical and Proven Exercises For The Mastery of True Self-Care

Marissa Leinart

Agape Publishing

©Copyright 2023 by Marissa Leinart - All rights reserved.

This document is geared towards providing exact and reliable information in regard to the topic and issue covered. The publication is sold with the idea that the publisher is not required to render an accounting, officially permitted, or otherwise qualified service. If advice is necessary, legal or professional, a practiced individual in the profession should be ordered.

All rights reserved.

The information provided herein is stated to be truthful and consistent, in that any liability, in terms of inattention or otherwise, by any usage or abuse of any policies, processes, or directions contained within is the sole and utter responsibility of the recipient reader. Under no circumstances will any legal liability or blame be held against the publisher for any reparation, damages, or monetary loss due to the information herein, either directly or indirectly.

Respective authors own all copyrights not held by the publisher.

The information herein is offered for informational purposes solely and is universal as so. The presentation of the information is without the contract or any type of guarantee assurance.

The trademarks that are used are without any consent, and the publication of the trademark is without permission or backing by the trademark owner. All trademarks and brands within this book are for clarifying purposes only and are owned by the owners themselves, not affiliated with this document.

This Workbook Belongs To

_____

Pledge

Today, I, _____ pledge to give my all as I journey toward becoming the best version of myself.

I pledge to put myself first, catering to my spiritual, emotional/mental, and physical needs before anything or anyone else.

Motherhood takes a lot from me, and it will be tempting to give up sometimes. But I choose to forge ahead - one small step after the other - regardless of setbacks.

I pledge to get my tasks done to the best of my abilities. When slip-ups occur, I dust myself off and keep moving.

I pledge never to give up on myself.

Contents

What Makes This Workbook Different — 1

A Message fom Marissa — 3

1. Chapter 1 — 5
   Help!

2. Chapter 2 — 17
   The Spirit, Soul & Body Connection

3. Chapter 3 — 29
   Time To Heal

4. Chapter 4 — 45
   Self-Discovery

5. Chapter 5 — 57
   Reflective Thinking

6. Chapter 6 — 73
   Effective Communication

7. Chapter 7 — 81
   Personal Development

References — 109

What Makes This Workbook Different

Hey momma!

Before you dive into the first chapter of this incredible workbook, I want to share an exciting promise with you.

By the time you complete this workbook, I guarantee you'll be bursting with motivation to put your newfound knowledge into action.

Believe me, you won't want to let this opportunity slip away!

Here's the thing: Information alone is valuable, but it truly comes alive when you combine it with application.

That's where the real magic happens, my friend.

It's all about transformation—unlocking your potential and unleashing your inner greatness.

To ensure that you can effortlessly apply everything you've learned, we've made it incredibly simple for you.

All you need to do is sign up for a free account on EvenBetter.app.

Once you're registered, we'll be right there by your side, offering guidance and support, helping you navigate the path that's best for you.

We're here to kick-start your journey towards becoming the absolute best version of yourself. And let me tell you, you absolutely deserve it.

So, without further ado, let's not waste any more time.

Take out your phone, **scan the QR Code** below, and let's embark on this incredible adventure towards a happier, healthier, and more fulfilling life.

This is the life you were meant to have, and together, we'll make it happen.

Are you ready to start your abundant life journey?

Let's do this!

Love you my friend.

A Message fom Marissa

Hey momma!

Thank you for continuing your self-care and self-love journey with me.

This workbook accompanies the book **Self-Care Self-Love For Overwhelmed Moms**.

For best results, please read it before using this workbook.

When I started writing the book **Self-Care Self-Love For Overwhelmed Moms**, I did not have a workbook in mind.

But the deeper I got into explaining each truth, the clearer it became that some moms would benefit from having a guide for deeper learning. My main reason for writing this material is to help moms become the best version of themselves through the **Mastery of Self-Care**.

This workbook allows you to pause and take a deeper look inside your soul. It also moves you to ask the most uncomfortable questions you might have ignored for many years.

And hopefully, it stirs you up to pursue your healing - spiritually, emotionally/mentally, and physically - at all costs.

As a woman with ten years of experience coaching and counseling parents in the United States and the Philippines, I come with a depth of knowledge. But my speaking, teaching, and coaching portfolio do not matter as much as my heart. So, from my heart,

I welcome you to this new journey as you step into the *"abundant life"* for which you were created.

Please note that if it all feels too heavy for you at any point, take some time off. Time off can be a few hours to a few days - but be sure to get back into it as soon as possible. If you have deep struggles continuing or do not have memories of your childhood, then it might be a sign that you need more support.

Love you my friend.

Chapter 1

Help!

> "It breaks my heart when I see a mom struggling to hold it together. And this gets more heart-wrenching when she has opportunities to lighten her load, but she finds it hard to ask or receive. It becomes inevitable that if you keep refusing help when needed, you will burn out."
>
> - *Self-Care Self-Love For Overwhelmed Moms*

Let's Examine The Word "Help"

To help means to assist or support. It suggests that someone or something more is needed to achieve the desired end. There are common areas where moms need help.

Checklist

Check the areas you need help with:
- Childcare
- Grocery shopping
- Cooking/Meals
- Cleaning
- Laundry
- Finances
- Making friends
- Sticking with plans
- Reaching my goals

Others:

Accept That You Need Help

Accepting help requires a lot of vulnerability, self-esteem, and humility. In the book, we looked at three categories of moms regarding accepting help; the 'independent' mom, the 'insecure' mom, and the mom-in-denial.

The 'Independent' Mom

Olivia is a work-from-home mom of two kids. She and her husband own a construction company not too far from where they live in Seattle. Olivia does the admin work for the company while she takes care of their two young ones. The first time we spoke, she lamented the amount of work she had to accomplish daily, making it hard to meet deadlines and follow up with customers, and the business suffered.

Olivia's husband had planned to hire an administrator - even though they had a tight budget - but she asked him to allow her to do the job because she was a well-trained administrator. And quite frankly, it was her way of doing something for herself other than being a mom. But it all proved too much.

"Marissa, I'm a mess! I need help!" Once my boys get up at 8 am, it is a rollercoaster of events till bedtime. I'm always moving from one thing to the next, cooking, cleaning, and eating. Then, there's work. I feel like I'm losing my mind. I can't continue like this. I need help."

Instantly, her countenance changed. I could tell her problem was not necessarily needing help but accepting it.

Olivia knew she needed help, but somehow, she found comfort in the daily grind of trying to do it all by herself. She subconsciously derived pleasure from it. Independence, in this sense, can be rooted in trust issues, pride, and more.

The "Insecure" mom

No one is born feeling 'less than.' Insecurities stem from various bad experiences, either from childhood or adulthood. The insecure mom finds
it hard to ask for and accept help because she feels she isn't worth it. She may have amazing people around her who can make her load lighter, but
she is crippled by low self-worth. She struggles daily to hold it all together while feeling stressed to the max.

The Mom-in-Denial

Denial is a classic defense mechanism. When a mom is in denial, she constantly ignores her reality to avoid addressing it. While it may
help her cope and 'autopilot' in the short term, eventually, stress will catch up, and she will reach breaking point. A significant problem with
constant denial of much-needed help is that you will end up mentally and emotionally drained. The impact will make it hard to connect with
your kids.

Exercise:

Now, it's time to turn inward and complete the exercises below.

What do you understand by the word "help?"

_____

_____

_____

Checklist

Use the list below to check off signs that you might be independent, insecure, or in denial about asking and accepting help:

Independent

- I tend to avoid being vulnerable
- My expectations of others are too high
- I've built high walls to keep people out
- I try to convince myself that its not that much work
- I am strong enough to do it all
- I feel proud of my self-driven nature
- I prefer to hide behind 'keeping busy'
- I think only about myself
- I struggle with perfectionist tendencies

- I associate asking and receiving help with weakness

Insecure

- I don't think I deserve help
- I feel scared, ashamed, or sick to my stomach when I try to ask for or accept help
- I fear being rejected or abandoned
- I think I'm just really shy
- I try to be perfect in my 'mom' duties
- I criticize my parenting a lot
- I prefer to be the helper than the receiver
- I compare myself with other moms who seem to be holding it together
- I don't believe I can do anything right – even asking and accepting helpI'm very self-conscious I find it hard to believe people really want to help

In denial

- I convince myself that I don't need help
- I avoid thinking about the daily grind of motherhood
- I avoid talking about the daily grind of motherhood
- I justify being woman enough to perform every task
- I point out other moms who are terrible moms (in my opinion)

- I ignore advice from family, friends, and loved ones, who tell me I need help
- I feel nothing

If you check most of the boxes in any category, then that category applies most to you. Sometimes, you can cut across more than one category. Whichever it is, don't beat yourself up. You're here to change these habits one step at a time.

Fill in the blanks:

Asking for help makes me feel...

_____

_____

because...

_____

_____

Accepting help makes me feel...

_____

_____

because...

_____

_____

Learning To Ask For and Accept Help

After establishing which category of mom you have been, it is time to learn how to ask and receive help.

Asking For Help

Know the **specific help** you need. Asking for help is easier when you have identified exactly what you need.

Know **who** can fulfill the need best. After identifying your need, consider who can give the best help.

Know the **time** to ask. Knowing who can help you is as important as knowing when to ask. While people generally love to help, it pays to give them time to process your request and respond.

Know **how** to ask. Asking involves communicating effectively. Choose words that the person will understand. Avoid beating around the bush.

Exercise:

Consider areas you have struggled with, and fill in the table below. To get started, see the examples provided.

Specific help I need	Who I will ask for it	When I will ask
Babysitting this Thursday night	Alicia (neighbor and mom friend)	Tonight (Monday)

Some Request Starters:

• I don't know if you are the right person to ask, but please could you help me with

_____

• I've been pretty stressed out lately, would you mind if I dropped my kid with you for a couple of hours?
• Could you do me a favor? I need:

_____

After following all the steps, your request will be granted or declined. If declined, don't take it personally or try to come up with reasons why.
Move on, and find other options.

Accepting Help

Sometimes, you may not need to ask before people offer to help. If you struggle with accepting help, try this exercise:

Exercise:

Stand in front of a mirror, look straight into your eyes and imagine someone is offering you help. Practice your response. Remember, your body language speaks just as loud as your words. Put on a smile, relax your shoulders and arms, and respond with:

- Thank you so much_____

- I would certainly appreciate that.

- Oh! How thoughtful of you_____
- Yes, please! You're a lifesaver!
- Without question, I accept.

The goal is to prepare your mind before you receive an offer of help. Practice these until accepting help graciously feels natural.

Self-Care Journaling:

Write down a heartfelt confession of your struggles as a woman and a mom.

_____
_____
_____
_____
_____
_____
_____
_____
_____
_____

What will you do differently today to be able to ask for and receive help?

_____

_____

_____

_____

_____

_____

_____

_____

_____

Chapter 2

The Spirit, Soul & Body Connection

> "Three vital parts - spirit, soul, and body are interconnected, so you cannot truly thrive if one or more components are deficient. Look at it as a three-legged stool. If one leg gets broken, your stance becomes shaky. All three must be intact and functioning to fulfill their purpose."
>
> - *Self-Care Self-Love For Overwhelmed Moms*

The state every woman should aspire to be is - **whole**. Wholeness means you are complete - not broken or fragmented. And this happens when your spirit, soul, and body are in a healthy place.

"Can I ever achieve wholeness?" Short answer: YES.

The Self-Care Self-Love For Overwhelmed Moms book looked at the healthy spirit, soul, and body connection and components.

THE SPIRIT, SOUL, & BODY CONNECTION

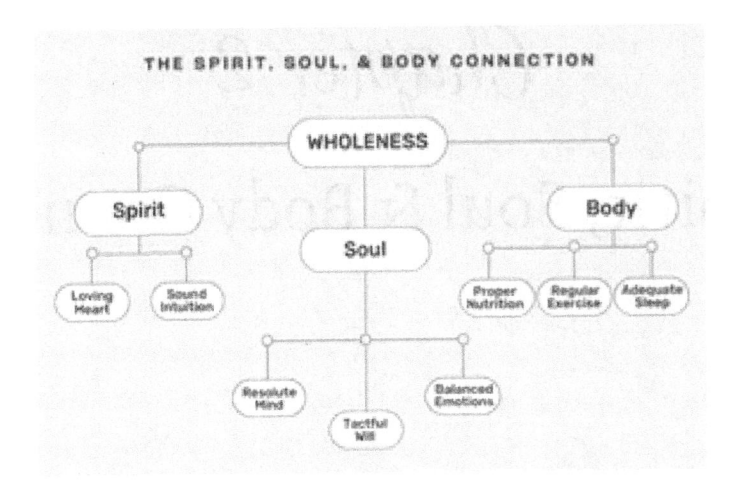

```
                        WHOLENESS
           ┌───────────────┼───────────────┐
         Spirit           Soul            Body
         ┌──┴──┐      ┌────┼────┐     ┌────┼────┐
      Loving  Sound  Resolute Balanced Proper Regular Adequate
      Heart Intuition  Mind   Emotions Nutrition Exercise Sleep
                        Tactful
                          Will
```

Exercise

Look at the Spirit Soul & Body Connection diagram and grade yourself on a scale of 1-5 for each component.

1 - Poor | This is a MAJOR struggle

2 - Fair | I sometimes struggle

3 - Good | I am just OK

4 - Very Good | This is my strong point

5 - Excellent! | I rock this like a NINJA!

Spirit

- I have a **loving heart** _____

- I have **sound intuition** _____

Soul

- My **mind is resolute** when it comes to:
  - Personal development _____
  - Fostering relationships _____
  - Raising/disciplining my kids_____
  - Community engagement _____

- I exert my **will tactfully** when:
  - Interacting with my kids_____
  - Interacting with my spouse/partner_____
  - Interacting with friends_____
  - Interacting with relatives _____
  - Interacting with colleagues_____

- My **emotions are balanced** _____

Body

- I eat **healthy foods daily**_____

- I **exercise regularly** _____

- I get **adequate sleep** _____

This is an assessment or snapshot of where you are today. It is not an exam to pass or fail. Doing this helps you identify improvement opportunities as you continue to become the best version of yourself.

Building Your Spirit

> A woman's spirit is fertile ground. All it needs is a tiny **seed**, a ray of **sunlight**, a splash of **water**, **nutrients**, and **time** to germinate. That seed is your *desire*. Your *determination, dedication,* and *discipline* are your sunlight, water, and nutrients. Then time will run its course, and the new you will be born. My seed (desire to come out of my terrible state) was all I needed to start, so I began my journey to activate my spirit-woman, keeping her alive and healthy, and from there, it began to flow to my soul, then my body.
>
> *- Self-Care Self-Love For Overwhelmed Moms*

Spiritual Exercises

These are activities to nourish your spirit, like meditations and prayers, reading scripture, and inspirational quotes.

Spiritual Meditation

Spiritual meditation is a type of meditation that helps you develop a deeper understanding of things of the spirit. It connects you with the Higher Power, higher consciousness, or self.

This type of meditation can lead you to experience a spiritual awakening, awareness, revelations, visions, sensing a presence, and so much more.

Everyone experiences this in their unique way. While some may feel a deep connection, others won't feel anything. You don't know when you will encounter a spiritual experience. Remain open and hopeful but don't try to force it.

Exercise:

A. Connect with God through prayers

- Ask for grace and strength to complete your tasks.
- Ask for wisdom in your role as a mom.
- Seek His counsel.
- Thank Him for answers to your prayers.

B. Connecting with a higher consciousness | self

- Start by setting a timer for this session. If you are new to this, five minutes is a good start.

- Sit quietly in a calm place. Ensure your sitting position is comfortable for you.

- Close your eyes and pay attention to the rhythms of your breath - in and out. You can place your right hand on your heart.

- Additionally, you can focus on a particular thought and go over it repeatedly. This thought must be positive, preferably of a desired area of personal development.

- If you notice your mind wandering, bring it back to the original focal point, which could be your breath or a thought.

- Take note of your body's sensations.

- When your timer goes off, exhale deeply, open your eyes, and sit still for a few more seconds before getting up.

Building Your Soul

> Your soul houses your mind, will, and emotions. It is essential that it becomes healthy and *stays* healthy. A healthy soul remains in a positive state regardless of the surrounding circumstances. The three components - your mind, will, and emotions - must all be well taken care of; otherwise, the intangible parts of your health will deteriorate.
>
> *- Self-Care Self-Love For Overwhelmed Moms*

Soul-Searching

Now and then, you'll need to do some soul-searching. Soul-searching involves deeply weighing your thought patterns, beliefs, mindset, and motives. It takes you on a path to answering questions about the state of your soul.

Soul-searching requires concentration (time to put that phone down!), complete honesty, and, most importantly, time. While it is a search for what's on the inside of you, some external factors can come into play, like reading spirit-lifting books and listening to music, podcasts, and messages.

Exercise:

Look within, think deeply, and answer the following questions. Remember, complete honesty with yourself will help you do this effectively.

What do you **love** about yourself? - Your character, personality, and looks.

_____

_____

_____

_____

_____

_____

What **don't you like** about yourself? - Your character, personality, and looks.

_____

_____

_____

_____

_____

_____

How do you describe yourself? Use the first words that come to mind.

_____

_____

_____

_____

_____

_____

What **ideas/thoughts** did you have about motherhood before you became one?

_____

_____

_____

_____

_____

_____

What **ideas/thoughts** do you currently have about motherhood?

_____

_____

_____

_____

_____

_____

Fill in the blanks:

Motherhood overwhelms me because:

_____

_____

_____

_____

_____

_____

Developing A Resolute Mind, Tactful Will, and Balanced Emotions

The **soul** (mind, will, and emotions) can be very temperamental. It takes patience and persistent focus to build it. Your aim should be to learn how to **regulate,** not **suppress**.

When you regulate, you are putting things under control. But suppression means you forcefully hide/keep something down. Think of these two elements as leaders. One uses a dictatorial leadership style, while the other uses a democratic style (not to be confused with a political party). Both leaders will give orders. The dictator demands compliance harshly and goes as far as using threats or worse. Fear rules the dictator's subjects. The leader using a democratic leadership style has a compassionate presence that compels people to comply without threats because they lead by example and serves the people. Who do you think will *genuinely* be respected? Chances are the leader with a democratic leadership style.

This leadership style example is similar to what happens with your soul. Your soul can learn to take control if you serve and teach it lovingly. Suppressing your feelings, emotions, or thoughts will only work short-term. So how do you regulate your feelings?

SOUL-care Strategy

There is an art to regulating, and I have developed a four-point strategy for this, which is called **SOUL**-care.

STOP: Make it a habit to make stops. It could be daily stops to turn off the many thoughts running through your mind. Momentary stops to exercise your will and navigate your emotions. It could be more organized stops to take time off to refresh your soul - detoxing from the noise of negative media. Just stop to take a few deep breaths! Avoid making any decisions and saying anything in the heat of the moment.

OBSERVE: Observe the sensations in your soul. Is your mind telling you the truth or those lies you have been accepting for years? Is your will geared towards proving your point because you have to be right? Are your emotions about to be triggered again? After stopping, observe what your soul is trying to communicate to you.

UNDERSTAND: Understand you have the power to choose your response to the feelings and emotions that you stopped to observe. Will you regulate your feelings and respond with compassion or react harshly?

LEAD: Take the first step and lead. Lead your emotions by choosing to respond with compassion, caring and kindness. This may take a while if you have built a lifetime habit of reacting harshly. Replacing one habit with another is intentional work. Take it one day at a time, one interaction at a time and you will begin to see progress.

When my kids were younger, there were a number of things that could easily get me worked up. My mind would dive into a thousand and one thoughts, emotions would be all over the place, and I would lose control over my will. A major one was getting my kids ready to go somewhere - the mayhem was intense. Once I mastered the SOUL-care strategy, rather than allow my soul spiral into a state of emotional/mental chaos, I would first STOP to just breathe, then I'll OBSERVE everything I'm feeling and thinking at that moment. Next, I UNDERSTAND that I have the power to choose how to respond to the scenario and not react. Then, that gives me the power to LEAD by speaking in a calm, caring yet firm voice to get their attention and get them out the door with all their school materials. No tears, no yelling, no running late because someone forgot something. Mission accomplished.

The impressive thing is once you get a hang of this from daily practice, this whole process could happen in a space of 10 seconds!

In the long run, don't wait for negative thoughts to bombard your mind before you take action. Be proactive and lead with positive thoughts from the moment you wake up. Let your mind, will, and emotions follow your leadership by always starting your day with meditation, reflective thinking, prayers, and affirmations.

Exercise:

Take 20-second stops at various intervals of your day. If you feel you are about to get overwhelmed, stop everything you're doing and just sit still.

Chapter 3

Time To Heal

> "A woman who is yet to heal will only be parenting from a place of hurt - and that is a very dysfunctional place to be. Women are life-givers. **Moms, for the most part, are responsible for the emotional atmosphere of the home.** We are the heart. And the nature God has given us that separates us from men is the ability to 'womb' and 'birth.' This is very powerful!"
>
> - *Self-Care Self-Love For Overwhelmed Moms*

Exercise:

Let's start with **your childhood**. Right now, clear every distraction, stay quiet for about two minutes, and think deeply about your childhood.

Start from your earliest memories, and answer the questions as you allow your consciousness to travel back to the subconscious.

What **age** were you in your earliest childhood memory?

_____

Where were you at that age?

_____

Who were the **significant adult figures** in your life then?

_____

What type of **emotions** are being evoked in you as you are answering these questions?

Circle **all** that apply; (Note that you can apply further qualifiers to these adjectives)

LOVE	HATE	HAPPINESS	NUMBNESS
SHAME	SADNESS	FEAR	GRATITUDE
JOY	DELIGHT	ANXIETY	SORROW
LONELINESS	ANGER	TRUST	DISGUST
CONTENTMENT	PEACE	SHOCK	MELANCHOLY
SATISFACTION	RAGE	SURPRISE	PRIDE

Now, answer these questions fully:

What positive/happy/pleasant childhood memories stand out most to you?

_____

_____

_____

_____

_____

_____

What negative/sad/unpleasant childhood memories stand out most to you?

_____

_____

_____

_____

_____

_____

Triggers: Evidence of Unresolved Trauma

> Triggers are your present expressions rooted in an experience of the past. It is usually an exaggerated response to an event in front of you. For instance, If you feel your heart racing faster, a surge of anger is welling inside you, or you are getting irritated whenever you hear your toddler whine or throw a tantrum, you have experienced a trigger. At that point, your anger is not because of your child's behavior but because you have unresolved emotions about *your* childhood.
>
> *- Self-Care Self-Love For Overwhelmed Moms*

Triggers are more common than we realize. Many of us constantly get triggered by our children's actions, and we don't even realize it. We have often only developed coping mechanisms to bury hurts from our childhood. Until we take the time to 'resolve' our past, we may not be able to identify what triggers us fully. After that, work can begin on overcoming them.

I started with the exercises above to make you take a mental trip back to your childhood. Most of who we are, how we act, and what we think about are rooted in experiences from our earliest memories.

Common Parenting Triggers

Many things can cause triggers in moms. Some of the most common ones include:

- Your child throwing tantrums
- Your child whining

- Your child being non-compliant or outrightly disobedient.

- Your child disrespecting you

- Your children fighting each other

- Your child playing with or wasting food

- Your child making a mess/playing

- Your child is refusing to share

You will know you are being triggered when:

- You give a disproportionate response | reaction to your child's actions/behaviors. For example, when your child throws a tantrum, rather than calm the child down and have a conversation, you get all worked up and have a meltdown and feel helpless.

- You feel very upset with something your child does or refuses to do, forgetting that kids would be kids most times. For instance, if your older child refuses to share a toy with a younger one, you feel extremely upset and always rush to intervene. This compulsion could be due to your childhood where you always felt cheated by your sibling, your parents always took your sibling's side, and vice versa, or other issues.

- You struggle to keep your emotions under control when relating with your kids.

- Your kid does things that cause you to suddenly want to slap, hit, or use abusive words at them.

- You suddenly feel like a conflict with your kid gives you deja vu moments.

In such instances, your reaction could be rooted in your memories of crying out for help and no one coming to your rescue or other issues from your childhood.

Exercise:

Use any of the emotions listed below to complete the following scenarios. Follow the pattern of the examples below. (Note that you can apply further qualifiers to these adjectives)

UPSET	AGGRAVATED	JUDGED	JEALOUS
DUMB	AGITATED	ANXIOUS	FRUSTRATED
ABANDONED	HELPLESS	CONFUSED	UNIMPORTANT
INVISIBLE	TERRIFIED	OVERWHELMED	ABUSED
RESENTFUL	CONFRONTED	SAD	USED
DISADVANTAGED	CHEATED	OUT OF CONTROL	GUILTY

Examples:

I feel **aggravated** whenever my teenage daughter **disrespects me**. It reminds me of how my mother always demanded respect from me and I had no choice but to give it to her.

I feel **helpless** whenever my toddler **throws a tantrum**. It reminds me of my childhood when I would cry for hours but no one came to my rescue.

I feel **guilty** whenever my kids ask for things I cannot afford. It reminds me of the **hardship I endured** growing up. So I borrow money to buy things I can't afford to please them.

Fill in the blanks:

I feel _____ whenever...

_____

It reminds me of...

I feel _____ whenever...

It reminds me of...

I feel _____ whenever...

_____

_____

_____

_____

It reminds me of…

_____

_____

_____

_____

Overcoming Triggers

Overcoming triggers takes time, so commit to it for the long run.

- Make it a habit to constantly pause and evaluate your emotions regarding certain behaviors/actions of your child.

Ask yourself: *What about my child's action reminds me of my own childhood?*

- If your child's behavior is harmful, disrespectful, or negative in any way, practice staying calm (you can take deep breaths before responding) first.

Then, remove your child from the situation or have a conversation with them when they are calm. If discipline is needed, do it in a calm and composed manner.

Forgiveness: The Pathway To Your Healing

> To forgive means that you make a **conscious decision** to let go of any feelings of resentment or retaliation against someone or a group of people who have caused you hurt (physically or emotionally). Forgiveness is not a feeling that the offender determines. You say that whether or not they deserve it, you **choose** to let go of the offense for your wellness.
>
> *- Self-Care Self-Love For Overwhelmed Moms*

The primary way to overcome triggers is to 'resolve' your past experiences. You cannot go back and change anything, and neither can I promise that you will forget everything negative that happened to you. But it is possible to work on yourself to the point where your scars do not define your actions. Forgiveness is your first step.

To forgive, you must **acknowledge** that you have residue of hurts, feelings of resentment, or bitterness. Sometimes, you may have lived on autopilot for so long that you easily miss signs that you harbor hurt and unforgiveness. I understand this because I was at this point many years back.

Checklist

Use the list below to check off signs that you need to forgive someone/some people and yourself:

Someone | Some People

- I experience frequent bursts of anger.
- I feel angry | vengeful whenever the person crosses my mind | I see the person
- I am triggered by certain behaviors | actions of my kids
- I blame the person| others for my ill feelings
- I find myself brooding over past negative experiences
- I find it hard to speak about any topic related to the person
- I speak negatively about the person and want others to do the same
- I wish evil for the person
- I am very uncomfortable around the person

I feel numb about the person or their well-being

Yourself

- I am overly critical of myself
- I keep thinking about past errors
- I self-sabotage
- I feel I don't deserve happiness or success
- The short time I allow myself to be happy is followed by much guilt
- I take the blame for everything - including things that were not my fault

- I never stop trying to be perfect

- I have lost touch with my wants/needs

- I find it hard to accept personal compliments | gifts/goodwill

- I feel the world will be better off without me

- I find it hard to make major decisions because I fear I might be wrong again

- I maintain an attitude that I obviously should have known better

- I feel numb about the person or their well-being

> "Heal: this process can take many forms but will always be a painful journey. Because, to heal, you will first have to bring back old hurt, look it in the eye, and talk about it with someone you trust. Reliving past pain will stir up trapped emotions, but the result is a much-needed release."
>
> - *Self-Care Self-Love For Overwhelmed Moms*

Exercise:

This is a follow-up from the first set of exercises in this chapter. But you can also use it if you have anyone else who has caused you deep hurt, even if they weren't a part of your childhood.

Use any of the emotions listed to complete the scenarios below. (Note that you can apply further qualifiers to these adjectives)

SAD	HEARTBROKEN	DISAPPOINTED	MISERABLE
SHATTERED	DEAD	CHEATED	RIPPED OFF
LET DOWN	TAKEN FOR GRANTED	LONELY	HURT
DISGRUNTLED	BRIBED	INFURIATED	ABANDONED
IRRITATED	HORRIFIED	NAUSEATED	USED
VIOLATED	NUMB	MALTREATED	OPPRESSED

Think deeply about the **person | people** that hurt you and the moment(s) you were hurt. Dig deep into those memories, and pour out your heart in writing, like you would if you had a therapist working with you. Be sure to hold nothing back. Once you are finished, sit there until you have the composure to continue the exercises.

Fill in the blanks:

I feel | felt when...

_____

does | did...

_____

The book highlights five choices you need to make to forgive and heal. Choose:

- – **Compassion**: this means choosing sympathy and concern over any kind of judgment.

- – **Perspective**: this means considering that you could have been the offender, so you forgive because you also wish to be forgiven.

- – **Release**: this choice is to release the offender from your grip.

- **– Love**: this is a choice to pour affection toward the offender - physically or from a distance.

- **– Giving**: this means choosing to give a gift to your offender. This gift could be material or a gift of prayers and good thoughts toward the offender.

Now go further. It is time to write your offender's name(s), pause, and consider what they may have had to deal with in their lives. It is a true saying that
hurt people often hurt people
. When you are finished, read it out loud for release.

Exercise:

Fill in the blanks:

You hurt me badly, but today, I choose to get out of my space and consider what you may have had to suffer in life...

_____

So today, I forgive you.

Go further to give a 'gift' to those still alive and within reach. This gift is totally up to you. It could be a physical/material gift or a gift of prayers for their well-being. Whatever you consider appropriate, please do.

If the person you need to forgive is **yourself**, then do this exercise:

Fill in the blanks:

I felt when I...

_____

_____

_____

_____

_____

_____

Now, stand in front of a mirror, look straight into your eyes, and repeat the words below:

Today, I choose to quit every self-judgment and self-deprecation. I refuse to stir up negative emotions about myself. I am taking daily steps to know the true me, and no matter how long it takes, I will discover her.

Fill in the blanks:

Write out words that you will now use to describe yourself.

I am...

_____

_____

_____

_____

_____

_____

So today, I forgive myself.

Most people are products of deep hurts and wounds. I am very grateful that you have made this bold step to find your healing so that you do not pass on your hurt/trauma to your children and others. Healing is not a small task and I commend you for your bravery.

Chapter 4
Self-Discovery

> "Simply put, self-discovery is the process of testing and examining who you truly are. At some point in motherhood, you may get to feel like you have 'lost yourself' - the only you that you know is the one who constantly gives all to care for and nurture your children."
>
> *- Self-Care Self-Love For Overwhelmed Moms*

In the book, we establish that the path to self-discovery involves asking three critical questions:

1. Who am I?

2. What am I here for?

3. What can I do effortlessly?

Exercise:

Who Am I?

The source of your life: Sketch your family tree. It doesn't have to be technical. If your family is large, you might name only the adults.

For example,

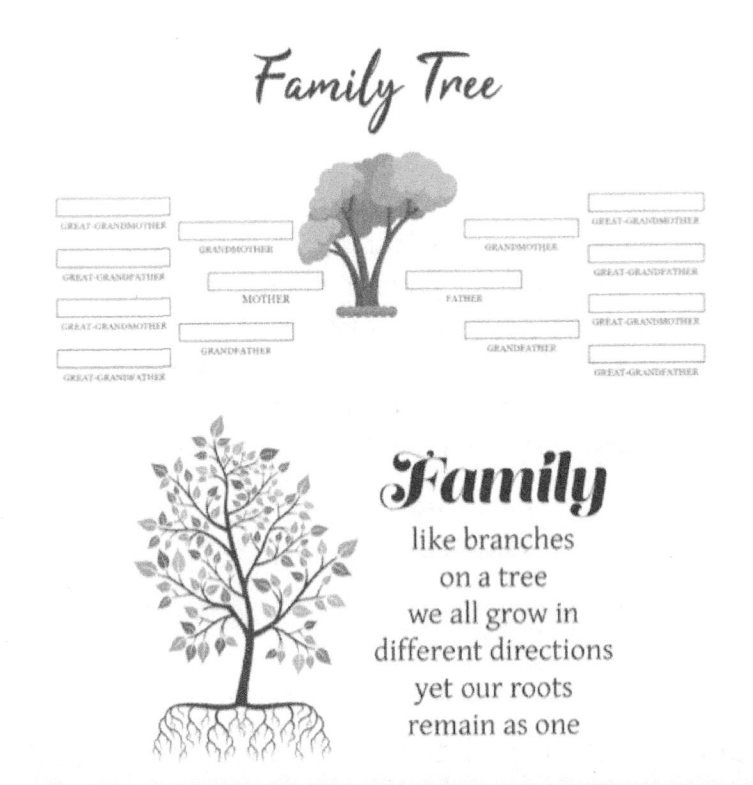

Family Tree

Family — like branches on a tree we all grow in different directions yet our roots remain as one

Draw yours here:

I come from an extensive family. My mom and dad each had six siblings! I don't know much about my dad's parents and relatives because they all lived back in the Philippines while I grew up in the United States. Even when I would visit, there wasn't much of an exchange because of the language barrier. But one thing was common; they all seemed emotionless. They lacked the ability to show affection and be sociable. They were cold and distant. And the truth is, that is how my dad was.

On my mom's side of the family, some undeniable traits ran across her, her siblings, and her parents. They were all extreme hoarders. This behavior was because of the hardship they had faced trying to survive after Japan attacked the Philippines. My aunt told me they had to live in caves and constantly flee from danger.

Unlike my dad's family, who were mostly uneducated, my mom's side was highly educated but had major anger issues. No one could even talk with a normal voice. It was constant yelling and screaming. My mom, however, was the 'quiet' one among them. This quietness was because she mastered the art of suppression. As the oldest girl in the family, it was her responsibility to take care of her younger siblings. So she had to learn to suck it up and just function. Her suppression of emotion was just as bad, if not worse, than yelling.

So, picture the product of these two families characterized by anger, coldness, and hoarding/ selfishness. Imagine a household where such vices controlled the atmosphere. Couple that with leaving a five-year-old to raise themselves. That was my life. No one needed to *teach* me *who to be*. I learned to *be like them* subconsciously. I learned to shut down and suppress my emotions rather than deal with them. I learned to function and perform on autopilot for my survival.

It took an intentional sit-down with therapists/ counselors to begin my healing journey and much more to get me to this wholesome place I am in today. And that is why I am very passionate about emotional health and healing, parenting from a whole and healthy state, and true self-care for moms. It gives me great joy to see a mom discover her roots as she works towards becoming the best version of herself.

You may have experiences similar to mine, or they may be different. If you feel you are doomed to continue a negative path, I am here to tell you that is not true. You can change your story! You can discover your **true self** - the person you were created to be, despite the trauma, hurt, misfortunes, and negativity that might have run through your lineage so far. Now, I challenge you to take the next exercise.

Exercise:

Ask your parents or older members of your extended family about their ancestry. Listen for the words they use to describe different members of the family and the experiences they have gone through. Knowing about your grandparents, aunts, uncles, cousins, and so on can help you understand why you act the way you do. It may even surprise you to discover traumas that may have been recurring through generations.

Fill in the blanks:

How do relatives describe my mother?

_____

_____

_____

How do relatives describe my father?

_____

_____

_____

How do relatives describe my (maternal) grandmother?

_____

_____

_____

How do relatives describe my (maternal) grandfather?

_____

_____

_____

How do relatives describe my (paternal) grandmother?

_____

_____

_____

How do relatives describe my (paternal) grandfather?

_____

_____

_____

How do relatives describe my...

_____

_____

_____

How do relatives describe my...

_____

_____

_____

Once you have filled in these blanks, analyze what stands out most, what seems to be shared (character traits, achievements, health conditions, etc.,) what complaints are common, what events have occurred repeatedly, and more. If it is too much to handle, you might need to work with a family therapist or counselor.

The characteristics of your heart: Remember when we treated the spirit, soul, and body connection. A loving heart is one of the two components of a healthy spirit. Take my **"Love Litmus Test"** below to know where you currently stand:

Circle either the left or right column to indicate where your heart is presently:

- When someone receives something you have been desperately desiring or hoping for your heart:

| Rejoices for them/is glad and content | Boil over with jealousy or envy/laments that you deserved it not them |

- When faced with a choice to sacrifice for others, your heart:

| Seeks the good and well-being of others | Seeks only yourself and insists on your way or the highway |

- When someone wrongs you, your heart:

| Forgives quickly | Is quick to get angry, hold a grudge/ imagines vengeance |

- When you acquire or are given something valuable or pricey, your heart:

| Feels humbled and privileged | Becomes proud and boastful |

- When you see someone is in need, your heart:

| Compassionately shows kindness | Is indifferent or judges them harshly |

- When there is wrongdoing and injustice, your heart:

| Aches and wants to correct the situation | Is indifferent or judges harshly |

- With delayed dreams, visions, and aspirations, your heart:

| Perseveres, remains hopeful and full of faith | Loses hope and gives up easily |

You may have worked it out that the left column signifies a loving heart, while the right one is still a work in progress. The truth is, we are all still a work in progress. These exercises help reveal where you currently are, so as to help you get to where you should be.

The state of your soul: This involves identifying the components of your soul; do you have a resolute mind, balanced emotions, and a tactful will? We covered this information in chapter two.

Exercise:

What Am I Here For?

Purpose seeks to answer the big question - what am I here for? I believe this should begin with a spiritual journey. Why? Because your purpose is more than what you see. Your talents are a clue to your purpose, but it is about more than natural abilities.

If you are yet to discover your purpose, start by including that desire in your prayers or meditation.

Now, answer these questions fully:

What am I most passionate (have strong feelings and intense emotions) about? Think deeply about the people you love to spend time with, the things that excite you, the places you have strong connections to, and your deepest desires.

_____

_____

_____

_____

_____

_____

What do I see that I desperately want to change in the world? Think about your past experiences - the ones you wish you could rewrite, the communities you are most drawn to, injustices that strike your heart repeatedly, and areas you struggled to overcome that you want to change.

_____

_____

_____

_____

_____

_____

What consistently inspires me to get up and get going? Think about your driving force, your primary motivation to become a better person, and the things you imagine yourself accomplishing before you leave planet earth.

_____

_____

_____

_____

_____

_____

Exercise:

What Can I Do Effortlessly?

Talents vary widely! And no list can give you every type of talent there is out there.

If you are still determining what you can do effortlessly, answer the question below:

What kinds of things come easily to you?

_____

_____

_____

_____

_____

_____

Think about those things you get done at such speed that other moms | friends | loved ones | colleagues have found challenging, solutions you come up with when others seem confused, and products you want to create.

_____

_____

_____

_____

_____

_____

If you find that you're still struggling to answer these questions, leave it for a while and get back some other time. Also, consider asking your friends, family, loved ones, and colleagues what they think your talents are. You may be surprised by their responses.

Chapter 5

Reflective Thinking

> "Reflective thinking is a consequence-based way of thinking. It involves carefully considering your actions or experiences, evaluating what you did, and why you did it. The lessons learned from it will lead you to decide what to do next."
>
> *- Self-Care Self-Love For Overwhelmed Moms*

Reflective thinking is a habit you should exercise daily, beginning in the morning. This way of thinking helps you become an all-around better person.

Ideally, you should get to a point where your entire being is under control - more loving and intuitive conversations and actions, less frequent outbursts and meltdowns, and wise choices with your physical well-being. But a mom's day-to-dayactivities can be unpredictable. You are thrown off balance again when you feel you've got the hang of something. Reflective thinking is a tool that helps you get back on track.

Reflective thinking is a common 'repair' method when actions need fixing. In truth, daily use of reflective thinking will give you fewer reasons to need to 'repair' your actions.

In the book, we listed three points to consider to reflect effectively; what you did, why you did it, and what to do next.

What You Did - Why You Did It - What To Do Next

When you need to make crucial decisions, solvea problem, repair a negative behavior, etc., the first thing to do is critically analyze your actions. Reflection works by looking at what you have done in the past and how it affected you so that you can evaluate what to do next. It can sometimes feel like a confession to yourself.

It can go something like this:

I dropped the ball today. My daughter took the car out without permission, and I yelled at her and called her names.

I've got to smash this presentation tomorrow!

The last time I led the team meeting, I was too nervous about getting all my words out.

This project is proving difficult. How can I connect the dots this time?

As moms, we are faced with decision-making daily. It could be for little things like what color of shoes the kids will wear, to bigger ones like what school your kids will attend. With big decisions, be sure to take time to reflect extensively.

Some big decisions include:

– Deciding to quit your full-time job to become a stay-at-home mom.

– Picking what school your children will attend.

- Deciding to become an entrepreneur.

- Hiring a caregiver for your infant | children.

- Moving to a new location.

- Starting your healthy lifestyle journey.

Exercise:

Use the questions below as a guide when making big decisions or solving a problem:

What is the issue | matter | subject?

_____

_____

_____

_____

_____

_____

What valid information do I have about this issue | matter | subject?

_____

_____

_____

_____

_____

_____

What are my thoughts and ideas concerning this issue | matter | subject?

_____

_____

_____

_____

_____

_____

Who else can give an opinion on this?

_____

_____

_____

_____

_____

_____

What is their opinion?

_____

_____

_____

_____

_____

_____

Who is affected by this decision?

_____

_____

_____

_____

_____

How will they be affected?

_____

_____

_____

_____

_____

What do I stand to gain with this?

_____

_____

_____

_____

_____

_____

What do I stand to lose with this?

_____

_____

_____

_____

_____

_____

Will I look back and be proud of this decision | action?   **YES | NO**

Is it worth it?   **YES | NO**

Use the questions below as a guide when reflecting on a behavior:

What did I do? Make your confession.

_____

_____

_____

_____

_____

_____

Why did I do it? Highlight surface reasons and underlying reasons. For instance, you got mad because your daughter spilled milk on the floor (surface reason). You are really mad because making a mess triggers you (underlying reason.)

_____

_____

_____

_____

_____

_____

What should I do next? After weighing your actions, and the reasons behind them, outline the next step to repair the damage.

_____

_____

_____

_____

_____

_____

Being a Present Mom

> "Your 'presence' is one of the most important things you can give to your child. This 'presence' transcends the physical but also the emotional. It means you take that specific time to cut out every distraction and give undivided attention to your child. You would think this should be easy, but in reality, the media, among other things, has made this a huge challenge."
>
> *- Self-Care Self-Love For Overwhelmed Moms*

Challenge:

I'm starting this section with a challenge. For 24 hours, switch off your cell phone, laptop | computer, and TV. The goal of this challenge is to let you see how attached you might be to these devices. The only personal items you can have close by are your workbook, journal, and pen. If you are a working mom, do this on the weekend. No excuses!

Depending on the age of your children, being present could mean different things and durations. Infants need lots of cuddles, young kids crave attention to chat and play, and preteens | teens | adolescents equally crave attention (though on their terms.)

Here are suggested durations for you to be fully present and bond with your child | children:

Stay-at-home moms of little kids	Work-from-home moms of little kids	Full-time working moms	All moms of adolescents
At least 2 hours daily	At least 90 minutes daily	At least 30 minutes daily	At least 15 minutes daily

Exercise:

Being fully present with a newborn/infant will involve holding your baby closely, giving eye contact, and cuddling. You can do this at different intervals. While feeding your baby, hold them close and speak/sing softly to them.

Below is a suggested daily schedule for moms of little kids, with highlights on how to be present during certain activities.

Stay-at-home moms of toddlers and preschoolers.

Aim to get up at least 30 minutes before your child. Spend time alone praying, meditating, reflecting, reading, journaling, or anything you consider important.

Time	Activity	Highlighted suggestions
Morning routine 7:30 am - 9 am	Make bed Dress up Have breakfast Brush teeth	If your little one can do these things by themselves, then just supervise. If they are unable to, assist. Sit together while having breakfast. Get everyone involved in clearing and cleaning up.
9 am - 12 pm	Kids learning time or work cycle (Academic activities)	At this stage, kids learn through play. Line up learning resources and materials for them to select what they want. Be fully present for at least an hour - showing them basic preschool learning, like the alphabet, numbers, shapes, and colors. Allow them to walk/play around the house when they need a break. You can use that time to do something for yourself.

Afternoon routine 12 pm - 1 pm	Lunch	Get your little one involved in making meals. Making simple meals together is also a way to bond. Sit and eat together. Doing this can help you model table etiquette and acceptable social behavior.
1 pm - 2 pm	Naptime/ Quiet time	Many toddlers and preschoolers still take naps. If yours has outgrown naptime, keep the schedule as "quiet time." Explain to your little one that they should play independently or quietly on their bed if they don't feel like napping. Utilize this time to do some laundry, take a nap if you need one, or do anything else.
2 pm - 4 pm	Playtime (Outdoors)	You can give your little one some screen time. Also, play outdoors - in your backyard or take a walk to the park. During this period, if you have an only child, you may need to join in on the fun. If they are more, you might only need to supervise.

Time	Activity	Description
4 pm - 5:30 pm	Snack More Fun activities/ Play (Indoors) House Chores	Offer your little one some snacks at this time. Avoid opting for only sugary stuff. Give fruits, nuts, and vegetables too! Then, let them have more indoor activities and involve them in basic house chores. Make it fun.
Evening routine 5:30 pm - 6:30 pm	Dinner Final clean up	Together, prepare dinner and clean up.
6:30 pm - 7:30 pm	Bedtime Routine: Bath Brush Teeth Book Reading Family Time Sleep	Bedtime is another great opportunity to be fully present with your little one. At this point, moms are usually exhausted, and we just move on autopilot. It will take a lot of strength and grace to slow down and be present. You can do children's bathing and brushing teeth with a bit of speed, but when it is time to read and tuck your kids to bed, slow down. Read softly to them and give hugs and kisses.

If you are a work-from-home mom, look for portions within your daily routine to turn off your devices and sit with your kids.

For full-time working moms, do everything you can to close early enough to meet your child's bedtime routine. Spend quality time - giving your undivided attention.

Moms of Adolescents; adolescents might act like they don't want you close but also crave quality time with you. Watch for their cues in conversations and join in willingly. Show interest in their school activities and hobbies. Show up every time they need your presence at school. Be friendly with their friends and the parents of their friends. A little effort goes a long way with teens.

Self-Limiting Beliefs

> "Self-limiting beliefs are the assumptions you have about yourself that hinder you from recognizing your true potential and achieving your goals... Self-limiting beliefs are often rooted in childhood experiences. They cripple you, and you find yourself stopping dead in your tracks when ideally, you should be progressing."
>
> - *Self-Care Self-Love For Overwhelmed Moms*

Exercise:

Our limitations are majorly in our heads. If we learn to come out of them, we can uncover our truest potential.

If you have goals to accomplish but constantly find yourself self-sabotaging, giving excuses, giving up, and abandoning things halfway, you might be limiting yourself mentally. Let's do some exercises to smash those self-limiting beliefs and get you closer to the best version of yourself.

Example:

I have been told several times that I should run for Mrs. USA. I imagine it sometimes, but I don't think I'm pretty enough. I think I can stay fit, but I'm not strong enough. I would probably give up by the second week, anyway.

Fill in the blanks:

I (state the self-limiting belief)

_____

_____

_____

_____

_____

_____

Next, reflect on why you hold this belief.

What experience(s) can you trace this to?

_____

_____

_____

_____

_____

Challenge:

You have identified the self-limiting belief, and you know it is only a lie. So, today, I challenge you to face your fears! The only way you can overcome limits is by pushing through them. After taking this challenge, write down what you did, and end by affirming yourself. Remember, this is only a first step. You will need to keep pushing through every day. Guess what? I know you can!

What I did today:

_____

_____

_____

_____

_____

_____

My Affirmations:

_____

_____

_____

_____

_____

Chapter 6
Effective Communication

> "Communication is said to be effective when both parties (speaker and listener) successfully exchange ideas and information in a clearly understood way. The result is usually mutual satisfaction."
>
> *- Self-Care Self-Love For Overwhelmed Moms*

Communicating effectively will be a major game-changer in your relationships. In the book, we outlined three questions your verbal communication should answer:

- Do my words convey what I have in mind?

- Am I using words that my listener is familiar with and will understand?

- What are my tone and pitch saying?

Exercise:

Example: *Assume you must discuss something sensitive | touchy with your spouse | partner. He is not very good at handling money. He splurges on extravagant things, and bills have been piling up lately. In your head, you want this conversation to end with him realizing he is wrong, apologizing, and possibly returning some things you consider unnecessary, then using the refunds to sort out bills. While you may not be able to predict his response, you can learn to communicate so that he is left with something to think about.*

What is the issue to discuss?

My husband spends on frivolous things and does not have enough for bills.

What do I want to achieve from this conversation?

My husband recognizes the negative impact of overspending unnecessarily, being remorseful, and changing his ways.

How will I achieve this?

I will communicate effectively.

After these questions, we can get into the nitty gritty of verbal and non-verbal communication. Please note that when having casual conversations, you may not need to ask these questions.

Your turn.

If you need to have a sensitive conversation with your friends, loved ones, relatives, and so on, or must reprimand or discipline your kids/teens, follow the pattern above.

Answer the following questions:

What is the issue to discuss?

_____

_____

_____

_____

What do you want to achieve with this conversation?

_____

_____

_____

_____

When bringing up a sensitive issue/topic with your spouse/partner, always start with reflective thinking. Analyze all you want to say, determine the right tone to deliver it. If you feel it is too touchy and may get you all emotional, write it out and read from it. That way, your emotions don't get in the way of your memory, and you can successfully deliver everything you have planned.

What will I say? Practice your tone and pitch; avoid using "you statements" instead, use "I statements."

For example, "This is how I feel when you...."

_____

_____

_____

_____

When bringing up a sensitive issue/topic with your spouse/partner, always start with reflective thinking.

Analyze all you want to say, determine the right tone to deliver it. If you feel it is too touchy and may get you all emotional, write it out and read from it. That way, your emotions don't get in the way of your memory, and you can successfully deliver everything you have planned.

What will I say?

Practice your tone and pitch; avoid using "you statements" instead, use "I statements."

For example, "This is how I feel when you...."

_____

_____

_____

_____

Active Listening

> "This communication skill involves being fully present when someone is talking to you. You go beyond just hearing the person's words to understanding the intentions behind the words. It also means you take away your judgment and opinions and simply listen to what they say. It sounds easy, but it takes a while to master it."
>
> *- Self-Care Self-Love For Overwhelmed Moms*

Speaking is just one-half of effective communication. The other half is listening. As written in the book, active listening techniques include:

- Being in the moment when having a conversation
- Showing that you're invested by maintaining eye contact
- Recognizing non-verbal cues
- Participating by asking relevant questions to keep the conversation going
- Paraphrasing what you've heard and reflecting on it
- Listening primarily to understand instead of to respond
- Holding back any judgment or advice

Exercise:

Following the example above about your husband/ partner not spending money wisely, let us assume their response is something like:

It's my money and you can't dictate how I spend it. Maybe you could find something to do from home to contribute financially and quit pinning all the bills on me.

Ouch! Let's practice our active listening skills. Answer the following questions:

– During conversations, be in the moment and show interest by maintaining eye contact.

- What hinders you from being in the moment when conversing with someone?

_____
_____
_____
_____
_____
_____

How can you take away those hindrances?

– Recognize non-verbal cues.

_____
_____

_____

_____

_____

_____

What is the other person's body language saying?

– Listen primarily to understand instead of to respond, participate by asking relevant questions to keep the conversation going, and paraphrase what you've heard.

_____

_____

_____

_____

_____

_____

What more do I want to know about this conversation? What exactly am I hearing him say?

_____

_____

_____

_____

_____

_____

- At this point, you will feel like you have a thing or two to snap back with but hold back any judgment or advice.

- Don't forget about non-verbal communication: let your body language and facial expressions be warm and welcoming. Try to release the tension from your face, especially when discussing something upsetting.

Don't wait for an issue to come up. Practice using these skills with your spouse today, using a topic you may have avoided discussing.

Hopefully, you and your spouse/partner will have more positive and less heated conversations as you hone your listening skills.

Chapter 7
Personal Development

> "No matter how big or small your dream is, you must have a plan that includes personal development. Becoming someone better will take personal growth - you need to identify your weaknesses and find ways to minimize them while leveraging your strengths. Personal development strengthens your character, which is foundational to your success. A strong character will sustain you at the pinnacle of your dream."
>
> *- Self-Care Self-Love For Overwhelmed Moms*

The essence of our **Self-Care Self-Love For Overwhelmed Moms** book set is to help you become the **Master of Self-Care**. And you can only achieve that by developing a habit of investing in yourself **daily**.

Personal development is your pathway to achieving this. There are certain traits everyone should work towards building, and as moms, we are no exceptions. Some of these traits include; discipline, determination, focus, resilience, gratitude, and responsibility.

Discipline

Let's focus on discipline.

Exercise:

Answer the following questions:

When you see the word "Discipline," what comes to mind?

_____

_____

_____

_____

_____

_____

Name three essential things you struggle to be disciplined with:

Struggle 1:

_____

_____

_____

_____

_____

_____

Struggle 2:

_____

_____

_____

_____

_____

_____

Struggle 3:

_____

_____

_____

_____

_____

Can you identify one thing in your life where you are disciplined? If yes, name it | them and why you feel you are disciplined with it | them.

_____

_____

_____

_____

_____

_____

Checklist

Use the list below to check off hindrances to discipline that apply to you:

• I am afraid - of the unknown, of the amount of work it takes, of what I might become, etc.

- I am lazy - my body, my mind, or my spirit is weak.

- I make excuses - I don't have the time, it's not the right time, I don't have the money, etc.

- Maybe I have the wrong belief/mindset - I can't do it, I'm not good enough, no one's ever done it in my family, etc.

- There are too many temptations around me - I don't live alone, other people tempt me, etc.

- I don't know how to go about it.

- I have little to no motivation.

- I'm not in the right frame of mind to take this on.

- My past hinders me.

- Others:

To build this trait, reflect on what you stand to benefit from it. For instance, when you develop discipline with your body (eating right and exercising regularly), you will be less likely to suffer from health issues, strong now and as you age.

Fill in the blanks:

For the three things you named, write out what you stand to benefit:

When I

I will benefit

When I

_____

_____

I will benefit

_____

_____

_____

_____

_____

_____

When I

_____

_____

I will benefit

_____

_____

_____

_____

_____

_____

Challenge:

It's time to act!
Answer the following questions:

What are the **exact - practical - immediate** steps you need to take to develop discipline in struggle 1.

For instance, if struggle 1 is *I am undisciplined with my time. I am always late for every appointment, which has affected my children too - they are always late for school!* The steps would be to create a daily routine for yourself and your kids that is easy to follow, set reminders on your phone, and paste some around the house.

_____

_____

_____

_____

_____

_____

Always refer to your written benefits when you need motivation. Building discipline takes daily practice and time. Begin with the little steps you can take immediately, then gradually move up to bigger ones. You can also have an accountability partner, mentor, or coach work with you.

Making Friends

> "Making friends is like any other life skill that takes practice - you try, fail, try, and try again. It may be easier for some than others, but it is possible for all. I believe we were created to have relationships with one another because we cannot get through life alone. When you are walking a tightrope, you need a safety net. That safety net is your circle of friends."
>
> *- Self-Care Self-Love For Overwhelmed Moms*

How To Make Friends

The book highlights five steps to making friends. **Go out. Be friendly. Meet up. Start investing. Give it time.**

Take a look at the differences between an acquaintance, a friend, and an inner-circle friend. Use this as a guide to answering the questions below:

Acquaintance	Friend	Inner-Circle Friend
Someone you know on a surface level	Someone you know well and share a bond with	Someone you know intimately and share a very strong bond with

Someone you do not interact with	Someone you interact with often	Someone you interact and spend much time with
Someone you are not obliged to help	Someone you often help	Someone you always come through for no matter what

Before you get up and go friend-fishing, start with this exercise.

Exercise:

Answer the following questions:

What is your definition of the word, "friend"?

_____

_____

_____

_____

_____

_____

_____

What are your core values? (what matters most to you in terms of making you feel happy, satisfied, and fulfilled)

_____

_____

_____

_____

_____

_____

Why do you need to make mom friends? (If you're not convinced you need them, you might struggle to put in your best efforts.)

_____

_____

_____

_____

_____

_____

What do you consider non-negotiable in friendships?

_____

_____

_____

_____

_____

_____

What will be okay to have in a friend?

_____

_____

_____

_____

_____

What would make someone qualify as an acquaintance rather than a friend?

_____

_____

_____

_____

_____

What is good to have in a friend? (think of what would make someone qualify to be a good friend)

_____

_____

_____

_____

_____

_____

What is great to have in a friend? (think of what would make someone qualify as an inner-circle friend)

_____

_____

_____

_____

_____

_____

Determining and writing your answers to these questions will help you set the standard for the type of friends you will make. See them as setting boundaries.

If you do not know what you want, you might end up in friendships you may not like. And remember, **be the type of friend you wish to have!**

Feedback:

After making a move, striking up conversations, and meeting up, take the time to write down your thoughts about your "new friends."

_____

_____

_____

_____

_____

_____

Fill in the blanks:

I met

_____

for the first time today, and I felt like

_____

_____

_____

_____

_____

_____

I met

_____

for the first time today, and I felt like

_____

_____

_____

_____

_____

_____

I met

_____

for the first time today, and I felt like

_____

_____

_____

_____

_____

_____

After a second meeting;

I met _____

again today, and I feel like

_____

_____

_____

_____

_____

_____

I met _____

again today, and I feel like

_____

_____

_____

_____

_____

_____

I met _____

again today, and I feel like

_____

_____

_____

_____

_____

_____

Life Planning

> "A life plan is a written document highlighting your goals (short and long-term) and vision, outlining how you intend to achieve them. It should consider unforeseen circumstances because life, as we know it, can be unpredictable. Hence, your life plan should be written in pencil and amended as you journey through the different phases of life."
>
> *- Self-Care Self-Love For Overwhelmed Moms*

MY LIFE PLAN

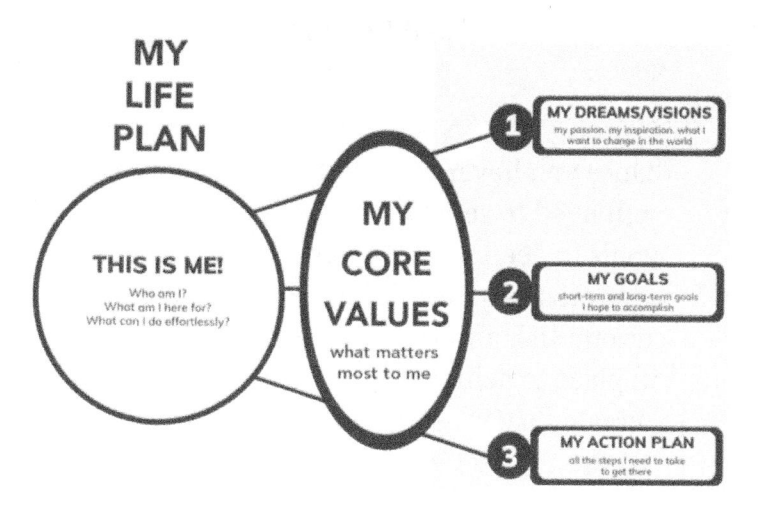

- **THIS IS ME!** Who am I? What am I here for? What can I do effortlessly?
- **MY CORE VALUES** what matters most to me
  1. **MY DREAMS/VISIONS** my passion, my inspiration, what I want to change in the world
  2. **MY GOALS** short-term and long-term goals I hope to accomplish
  3. **MY ACTION PLAN** all the steps I need to take to get there

Exercise:

Identify your core values - what matters most to you in terms of making you feel happy, satisfied, and fulfilled. (Your core values will be the main driving force to achieve your goals)

_____

_____

_____

_____

_____

_____

Your dreams/visions connect to your purpose. We covered this in the **Exercise: What Am I Here For** section of Chapter 4.

Goal Setting

> "Once you have identified your dream, you will need to set short-term and long-term goals to keep you on track. Goal setting is a process of determining what you want to accomplish and the measures you will put in place to achieve them. George T. Doran created a goal-setting technique known as the SMART goals. SMART stands for Specific, Measurable, Assignable, Realistic, and Time-related. This technique can be used mainly for your short-term goals."
>
> *- Self-Care Self-Love For Overwhelmed Moms*

Exercise:

S.M.A.R.T. Goals

Answer the following questions:

Specific: What is that specific area that you are out to improve? What exactly do you want to achieve?

_____

_____

_____

_____

_____

Measurable: What can you complete within a set time? Make sure there are parameters to measure your progress for every phase.

_____

_____

_____

_____

_____

_____

Assignable/Achievable: Who will do what? In this case, you are the one taking action. What can you accomplish or assign within a specific timeframe?

_____

_____

_____

_____

_____

_____

Realistic/Relevant: What can you achieve with the available resources?

_____

_____

_____

_____

_____

_____

Time-related: When will you achieve your desired results?

_____

_____

_____

_____

_____

_____

For your long-term goals: You can make 12 copies of this page to set short-term goals for each month of the year. They will all tie up in the long run.

Exercise:

Your Action Plan

In the main book, we highlighted three things that must be reflected in your action plan:

- The **tasks** you will be doing
- The **resources** you need
- Within the **timeline** for completion.

Fill in the columns:

When you have your goals written out, consider the three aspects of action planning and make a framework.

Answer the following questions:

- What tasks will I need to do to get closer to my goals?

What resources will I need for each phase of my goals?

_____

_____

_____

_____

_____

_____

How long will it take to complete each task?

_____

_____

_____

_____

_____

_____

Now, put it all together by filling this table:

Tasks	Resources	Start date	Due date

Life Planning For Your Kids

Have you talked with your kids about their life plans? Life planning helps them activate their imaginations about the future, and it's fun.

Activities:

For kids ages 2-5: sit with your toddlers or preschoolers and choose an activity.

A. Sketch how you see yourself when you grow up.

B. Paint a picture of yourself when you are a lot older.

C. Draw yourself doing things you love. (Mom, sketch yourself holding your baby, baking, holding office files - whatever your job/interests are.)

Writing Your Eulogy

> "If you carefully consider that your life has an end, you may get some motivation to stop procrastinating and chase your dreams. Life is short and goes by quickly. Think about when you were in middle school and how it felt like those days would never end. But here you are in your 20s, 30s, 40s, or even 50s—many years passed by like a flash. Taking time to reflect on your passing could give you a new perspective on the brevity of life and provide the motivation you need to get up and get going with whatever you can work with now."
>
> *- Self-Care Self-Love For Overwhelmed Moms*

Exercise:

Your Eulogy

In the book, we stated that when writing your eulogy, start with a draft highlighting three things:

- Who you were
- The people that mattered
- What you accomplished

Fill in the blanks:

– Who you were.

When and where were you born? What kind of personality did you have? What were your hobbies, likes, and dislikes?

_____

_____

_____

_____

_____

_____

– The people that mattered.

What was your relationship status? What influences did family, friends, and loved ones have on you throughout your life's journey?

_____

_____

_____

_____

_____

_____

– What you accomplished.

How would you describe your role as a mom?

What were your career, business, or charity/non-profit accomplishments? What impacts did you make beyond your immediate community?

_____
_____
_____
_____
_____
_____

– Your final words.

Talk about what you pass on to the next generation (material and moral legacies).

End with gratitude for living a rich and fulfilling life, and leave your family members with the assurance that your presence will always be with them.

_____
_____
_____
_____
_____
_____

As a creative tip, you can record a final video for your family members and loved ones and let them know where you keep it.

But insist that it is only played after your passing.

Final Words

It is easy to think that transformation and healing can happen in a flash, but this is rarely the case. We are all products of many years of various levels of experiences that have shaped what we believe (about ourselves, others, and the world) and how we think and act.

True transformation is a journey. The healing that leads to wholeness is a journey. See your life as a journey toward excellence. My journey began 20 years ago and continues as long as I have breath.

You have all it takes to discover what you were created for and walk on the path of your destiny. You have everything in you to take hold of your dreams and turn your life around. The only person who can stop you is YOU.

A life of abundance is waiting for you; abundance is in your spiritual, mental, and physical health. It is your responsibility to get up and claim it!

I have loved every moment spent bringing you the truths I have learned as a woman and mom. I genuinely hope that you start now to create a new and redeeming path for yourself.

NEXT STEP
I've loved sharing my truths with you!

Now, it's time for you to create a new and fulfilling path for yourself.

If you're starting your self-discovery journey or already familiar with soul-searching, I've got something special for you: the **EvenBetter.app**

It's designed just for you by me and my developer!

No matter if you're coasting or need help with managing your emotions, this app has it all.

Journaling, life planning, group coaching, life scoring, and a private community available 24/7.

It's your key to calming down, gaining self- awareness, and connecting with others who get it.

So, scan the QR code below or go to EvenBetter app.

It's time to uncover your true self and create a life that speaks to your soul. Let's do this!

Love you, my friend,

Marissa Leinart

me@AboutMarissa.com | me@EvenBetter.app

References

Chapter 1

https://www.verywellmind.com/denial-as-a-defense-mechanism-5114461

https://mindyourmamma.com/self-care-development/living-life-on-autopilot/

https://www.insider.com/guides/health/mental-health/insecurity

https://www.mindbodygreen.com/articles/signs-you-dont-love-yourself

https://www.northpointrecovery.com/blog/10-signs-serious-denial/

https://voi.id/en/lifestyle/98430/recognize-the-7-signs-of-denial-syndrome-the-habit-of-denying-statements-to-avoid-anxiety

https://psyche.co/guides/how-to-ask-for-help-without-discomfort-or-apology

Chapter 2

https://www.healthline.com/health/mind-body/spiritual-meditation

https://www.artofliving.org/us-en/blog/what-is-spiritual-meditation-experience-the-power-of-human-spirit-now

Chapter 3

https://positivepsychology.com/positive-negative-emotions/

https://onetimethrough.com/what-you-need-to-know-about-parenting-triggers/

https://timesofindia.indiatimes.com/readersblog/parenting-journey/how-to-identify-parenting-triggers-and-10-ways-to-deal-with-them-41867/

https://genmindful.com/blogs/mindful-moments/why-do-my-kids-trigger-me

https://www.spirituallivingforbusypeople.com/unforgiveness

https://kainosproject.com/2018/11/08/forgiveness/

https://www.baggagereclaim.co.uk/11-signs-youre-withholding-self-forgiveness-and-being-super-hard-on-yourself/

https://vickiechampion.com/2019/03/15/15-signs-you-have-not-forgiven-yourself/

https://www.healthline.com/health/list-of-emotions
https://www.verywellmind.com/what-is-compassion-5207366

Chapter 4

Scriptural References: I Corinthians 13:1-7

Chapter 5

https://blog.speak-first.com/the-7-questions-to-improve-your-decision-making-and-critical-thinking
https://www.parents.com/parenting/better-

parenting/teenagers/ways-to-connect- better-with-your-teen/
https://www.kidshealth.org.nz/parenting-teens- spending-quality-time-together

Chapter 7

https://www.successconsciousness.com/blog/ inner-strength/lack-of-self-discipline/
https://www.indeed.com/career-advice/ career-development/discover-core-values
https://www.lssu.edu/wp-content/uploads/2021 /09/SMART-Goals-Worksheet-1.pdf

Made in the USA
Middletown, DE
22 December 2024